To:

_____

You are one of the best things to happen in 1994.

And, as you are about to discover - a whole bunch of other historic events occurred in 1994 too! Enjoy!

Best wishes from:

_____

'That day, for no particular reason, I decided to go for a little run. So I ran to the end of the road. And when I got there, I thought maybe I'd run to the end of town. And when I got there, I thought maybe I'd just run across Greenbow County.
And I figured, since I run this far, maybe I'd just run across the great state of Alabama. And that's what I did. I ran clear across Alabama.

For no particular reason I just kept on going. I ran clear to the ocean. And when I got there, I figured, since I'd gone this far, I might as well turn around, just keep on going. When I got to another ocean, I figured, since I'd gone this far, I might as well just turn back, keep right on going'.

— Forrest Gump

EVENTS THAT TOOK PLACE IN
JANUARY

Top Songs across the UK and USA charts this month:

United States: "Hero" by Mariah Carey
United Kingdom: "Mr. Blobby" by Mr. Blobby

BORN IN 1994

Events that took place in the UK

The Duchess of Kent joins The Roman Catholic Church – the first member of the Royal Family to do so in more than three hundred years.

Jayne Torvill and Christopher Dean win the British ice dancing championship in Sheffield.

They attempted to replicate their Olympic success with their awe inspiring Bolero routine.

Prince Charles, aged 57 retires from playing polo after a 40 year playing career.

There is footage of him playing with the Duke of Edinburgh during the Commonwealth Games in 1966.

BORN IN 1994

- **Sir Matt Busby, iconic Manchester United Manager dies at the age of 84.**
  He lived long enough to see the world-famous club he built end their 26-year wait to be crowned English champions again.

- **British Aerospace sells its 80% stake in car maker Rover to BMW leaving the UK without a domestic car-maker.**

  Labour Leader John Smith strongly criticises the sale.

- The ailing Conservative Government is twenty points behind labour despite an improving economy and lower unemployment.

- British comedy "Four Weddings and a Funeral" written by Richard Curtis, starring Hugh Grant premieres at the Sundance Film Festival.

BORN IN 1994

Events that took place in the US

• In a historic event US President Bill Clinton meets with Russian President Boris Yeltsin.

They agree the 'Kremlin Accords' which attempts to de-escalate ongoing nuclear tensions.

During a lighter moment in their professional relationship it was reported that Yeltsin drank too much and apparently wandered into the street in his underwear trying to buy a pizza.

BORN IN 1994

US Vice President Al Gore oversees a meeting about the growing 'Information Superhighway' in the United States. This was the precursor to today's internet.

Super Bowl XXVIII

The Dallas Cowboys beat the Buffalo Bills 30-13.

Record cold temperatures hit the Eastern United States.

The lowest temperature seen in Sussex County, New Jersey, was −26 °F (−32.2 °C) on January 21, 1994.

BORN IN 1994

THE KERRIGAN VS HARDING SCANDAL

In a scandal that reverberated around the world, Figure Skater Nancy Kerrigan was assaulted by the partner of her rival Tonya Harding.

Both the assailant and Harding's ex-husband were jailed for the assault.

Nancy was the only skater in Tonya Harding's way to win the Gold Medal.

Look for the skates to follow this drama!

8

BORN IN 1994

EVENTS THAT TOOK PLACE IN
FEBRUARY

Top Songs across the UK and USA charts this month:

USA: "All For Love" by Bryan Adams, Rod Stewart & Sting
United Kingdom: "Things Can Only Get Better" by D:ream

BORN IN 1994

Events that took place in the UK

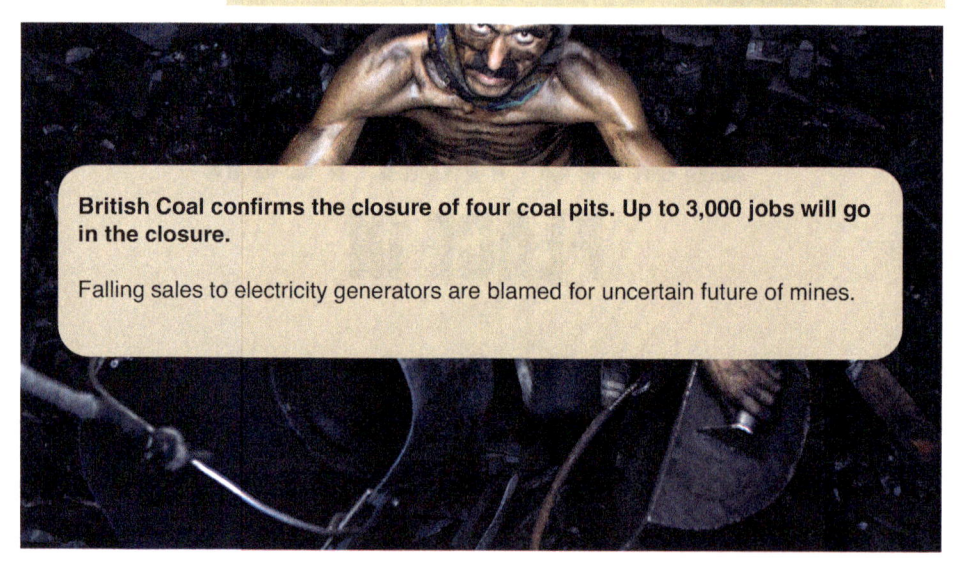

British Coal confirms the closure of four coal pits. Up to 3,000 jobs will go in the closure.

Falling sales to electricity generators are blamed for uncertain future of mines.

Conservative MP, Steven Milligan is found dead of asphyxiation. It is believed that his death was as a result of an intimate act.

Honda sells its remaining stake in the Rover Group allowing BMW full control over the brand.

BORN IN 1994

● **Great Britain & Northern Ireland compete at the Winter Olympics in Lillehammer, Norway.**

Jayne Torvill and Christopher Dean win a Bronze medal for their infamous figure skating and Nicky Gooch - a bronze for short track speed skating.

Police begin excavations at 25 Cromwell Street, Gloucester – the home of Fred & Rosemary West over the disappearance of their daughter Heather.

Days later, Fred is arrested over the murder of his daughter and that of another young woman, Shirley Robinson.

BORN IN 1994

Events that took place in the US

American rock band Green Day release their breakthrough album Dookie.

The album was originally titled 'Liquid Dookie'

Green Day's Billie Armstrong shared in a documentary that writing some of the songs for Dookie helped soothe his troubled mental state.

Song-writing was a way to deal with his severe anxiety, panic attacks and residual anxiety - all of which are results from his troubled childhood and losing his father when he was only 10-years old.

Dookie's commercial success propelled punk into the mainstream, but it also brought new challenges for the band as they all experienced an 'identity crisis'.

BORN IN 1994

In Oregon, figure skater Tonya Harding is charged with having her ex-husband assault rival Nancy Kerrigan.

United States F-16 pilots shoot down four Serbian fighter aircraft over Bosnia and Herzegovina after breaching a no fly-zone.

President Bill Clinton lifts the 19-year U.S. trade embargo against Vietnam.

This was due to Hanoi cooperating with American forensic teams when trying to identify and locate the missing 2,238 US personnel listed as missing in Vietnam.

13

EVENTS THAT TOOK PLACE IN

MARCH

Top Songs across the UK and USA charts this month:

United States: "The Power Of Love" by Celine Dion
United Kingdom: "Without You" by Mariah Carey

BORN IN 1994

Events that took place in the UK

● **IRA launch first of three mortar attacks on London's Heathrow Airport.**

On March 9th 1994, the IRA launched five mortar bombs towards Heathrow Airport's northern runway, preceded by a coded warning given an hour earlier. This incident marked the beginning of three separate IRA mortar assaults on the airport within a five-day period, during which none of the shells detonated.

Police confirm that they have found eight bodies buried at 25 Cromwell Street - the home of now infamous Fred and Rose West.

After police found human remains and apparent signs of torture at 25 Cromwell Street, Rose, along with Fred, was arrested in February.

● **BBC Radio Five Live broadcasts for first time in United Kingdom**

15

BORN IN 1994

The Church of England ordain women as priests for the first time.

The very first being Angela Berners-Wilson.

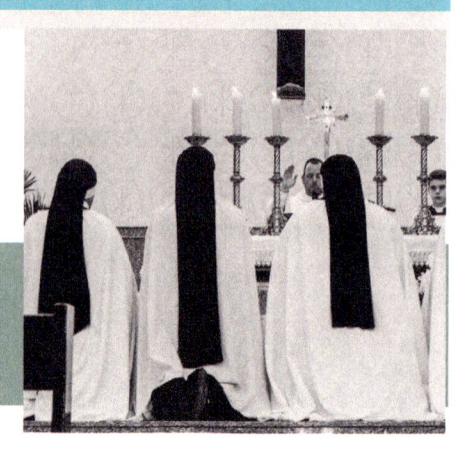

One of the UK's number one theme parks, Alton Towers, opens 'Nemesis' - Europe's first inverted roller-coaster.

In Rugby Union, England beat Wales, 15-8 at Twickenham, London but the Welsh take the Five Nations Rugby Championship as the title was decided by using points difference for the first time.

BORN IN 1994

Events that took place in the US

Nirvana play their final concert.

The 66th Academy awards is hosted by Whoopi Goldberg in Los Angeles.
Steven Spielberg's 'Schindler's List' wins seven Oscars including Best Picture and Best Director.

In Oregon, Tonya Harding pleads guilty for trying to cover up the attack on her rival, Nancy Kerrigan. She is fined and banned from the sport.

BORN IN 1994

US Defence Department announces smoking ban in workplaces.
The move was aimed at protecting non-smokers from second-hand smoke and creating a healthier work environment.

Two military aircraft collide in North Carolina killing 24 and injuring over 100 people.

A huge tornado destroys a Methodist church in Alabama killing twenty two people.

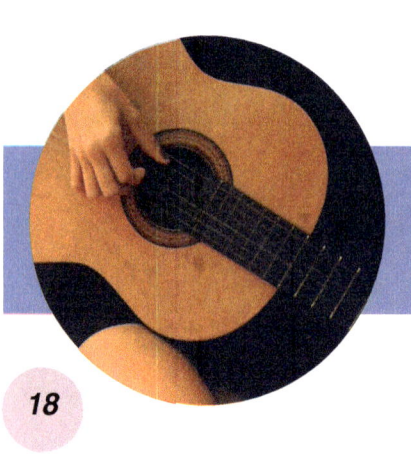

Singer songwriter Gloria Estefan is awarded the first Latin Walk of Fame in Miami.

BORN IN 1994

NASA STS-62 Launched A Shuttle Mission.

The Space Shuttle Columbia launched from the Kennedy Space Centre.

The crew of five tried growing crystals in microgravity as part of their experiments.

"Little More Magic" opens at Belasco Theatre NYC for 30 performances.

The Belasco Theatre is a historic Broadway theatre located in Manhattan, New York City. It has been the venue for numerous significant plays and musicals throughout its history.

19

BORN IN 1994

EVENTS THAT TOOK PLACE IN

APRIL

Top Songs across the UK and USA charts this month:

United States: "The Sign" by Ace of Base
United Kingdom: "Doop" by Doop

BORN IN 1994

Events that took place in the UK

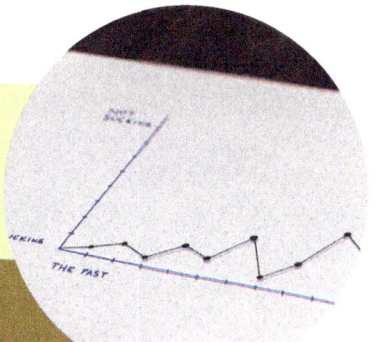

- **Economic growth in the UK shows the highest quarterly increase in five years.**

  Unemployment also falls to 2.5 Million as the UK recovers from recession.

- **Opinion polls show that support for the Conservatives has fallen to only 26% - their worst result in their whole 15 years in power.**

- **Remains are found in a field in Gloucestershire by police investigating the Fred West murders.**
  The body is believed to be Fred West's first wife. Fred's second wife, Rosemary is later arrested and charged with the murder of three of the victims.

- **Women's Royal Air Force fully merged into Royal Air Force.**

BORN IN 1994

Events that took place in the US

- Kurt Cobain of Nirvana commits suicide at his home in Lake Washington.

- The heads of the main tobacco companies testify before a House subcommittee that tobacco is not addictive.

- Former President Richard Nixon suffers a stroke and dies 4 days later, aged 81. He receives a state funeral.

- Rodney King is awarded $3.8 Million compensation by Los Angeles County having been beaten by police officers.

- Arsenio Hall announces he will end his late-night TV talk show in May 1994.

BORN IN 1994

EVENTS THAT TOOK PLACE IN

MAY

Top Songs across the UK and USA charts this month:

United States: "Bump N' Grind" by R. Kelly
United Kingdom: "The Most Beautiful Girl In The World" by Symbol

EVENT SPOTLIGHT:
MICHAEL JACKSON & LISA PRESLEY'S WEDDING

The King of Pop Michael Jackson and Lisa Marie Presley, the only daughter of Elvis Presley shocked the world when they announced their marriage - their relationship had been a well kept secret until that point.

The couple married on May 26, 1994, in a private ceremony in the Dominican Republic, away from the media spotlight.

Many speculated about the authenticity of their romance, with some suggesting it was a publicity stunt. However, both Jackson and Presley insisted that their relationship was genuine and based on love.

Following their marriage, the couple made a notable appearance at the MTV Video Music Awards in 1994, where they publicly kissed.

The marriage was relatively short-lived. They divorced in early 1996, citing irreconcilable differences. Despite the divorce, Presley later stated that she and Jackson had maintained an on-and-off relationship for several years following their separation.

"If I ask you to marry me, would you do it?" asked Michael on the phone one day.

"I would do it" said Lisa Presley.

BORN IN 1994

Events that took place in the UK

- Police find further remains at a previous home of Fred West. The remains are believed to be those of his daughter.

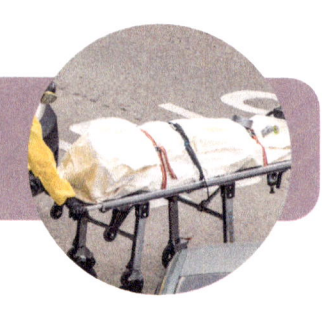

- Local council elections see the Conservatives take a battering. Labour gains significantly.

The Channel Tunnel opens for the first time between France and England.

BORN IN 1994

- Labour Leader, John Smith dies suddenly from a massive heart attack.

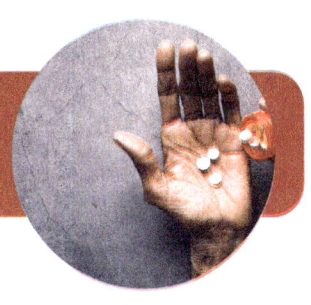

- Camelot Group wins the first ever contract for the National Lottery.

- Labour's Tony Blair and Gordon Brown meet to discuss who will be the next Labour leader and potentially the next Prime Minister of the UK.

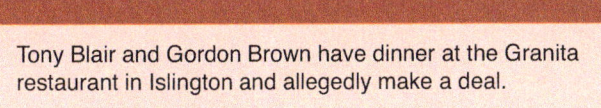

Tony Blair and Gordon Brown have dinner at the Granita restaurant in Islington and allegedly make a deal.

- The 34th European Cup Winners Cup is won by Arsenal after they played Parma, Italy in Copenhagen.
Arsenal defeated Parma 1-0.

BORN IN 1994

Events that took place in the US

Former First Lady Jacqueline Kennedy Onassis dies at the age of 64.

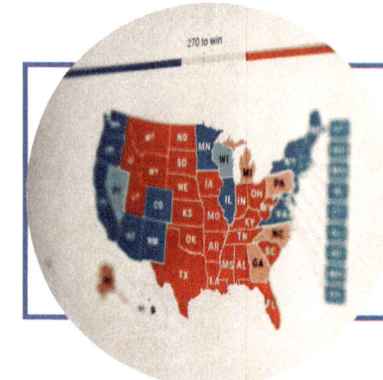

President Clinton and his party suffers a surprise electoral defeat in the State of Kentucky.

Serial killer John Wayne Gacy is executed for the murder of 33 young men and boys.

BORN IN 1994

Final episode of American TV drama "LA Law" after 8 year run.
"L.A. Law" first aired in 1986 and quickly became known for its ensemble cast, complex legal cases, and its blend of drama and humour. The show was set in a fictional Los Angeles law firm and tackled various legal and social issues.

"The Flintstones" live action movie based on the 1960s cartoon, starring John Goodman (as Fred), Rick Moranis (as Barney), and Rosie O'Donnell (as Betty) premieres.

EVENT SPOTLIGHT:
NELSON MANDELA'S ELECTION AS A PRESIDENT OF SOUTH AFRICA

His election marked the end of the apartheid era in South Africa, a system of institutionalised racial segregation and discrimination that had been in place since 1948.

Mandela was elected in South Africa's first fully representative democratic election. Prior to this, the country's black majority had been excluded from the political process.

Mandela spent 27 years in prison for his activism against the apartheid regime, becoming an international symbol of resistance to oppression.

The election took place from April 27 to April 29, 1994. April 27 is now celebrated as Freedom Day in South Africa, commemorating the first post-apartheid elections held on that day.

Mandela created a diverse government, called the Government of National Unity, which brought together politicians from different parties. This even included members from the National Party, the party that had previously enforced apartheid.

Mandela's presidency and his broader life's work left a profound impact on South Africa and the world. He is celebrated globally as a symbol of peace, reconciliation, and the struggle for freedom and equality.

EVENTS THAT TOOK PLACE IN
JUNE

Top Songs across the UK and USA charts this month:

United States: "I Swear" by All-4-One
United Kingdom: "Come On You Reds" by Manchester United FC & Status Quo

BORN IN 1994

Events that took place in the UK

Fred West is formally charged with eleven murders whilst his wife, Rosemary is charged with the murder of nine young women over a twenty year period.

- The Conservative Party suffer their worst defeat this century in European elections. Labour continue to surge ahead despite not having a leader.

- Railway workers go on strike closing down the rail network.

- Sir Norman Fowler resigns as Chairman of the Conservative Party.

BORN IN 1994

Events that took place in the US

Walt Disney Pictures releases 'The Lion King' to critical acclaim.
It is the highest grossing film of the year and at the time was the highest grossing animated film of all time.

- In the 1994 Stanley Cup, the New York Rangers are crowned as Ice Hockey champions.

- The 1994 FIFA Soccer World Cup begins in the United States.

34

BORN IN 1994

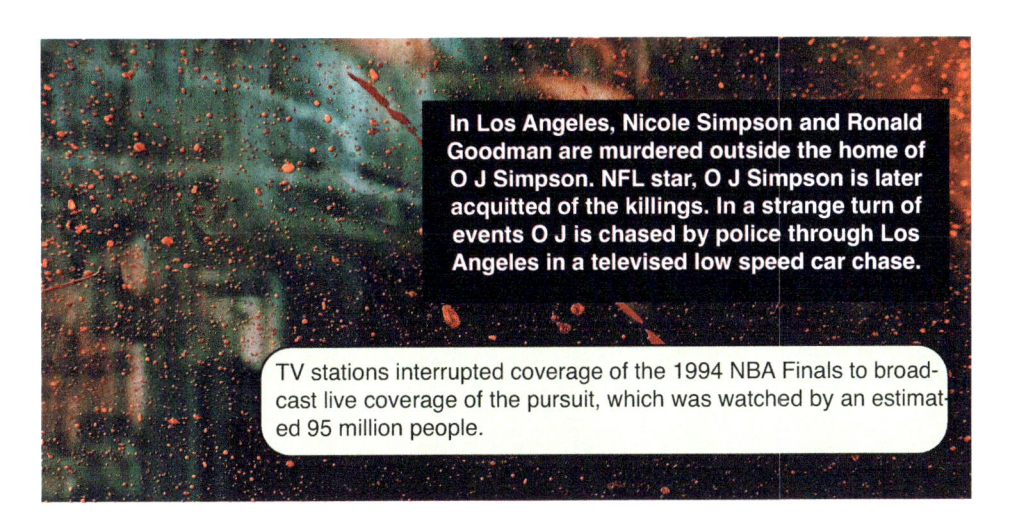

In Los Angeles, Nicole Simpson and Ronald Goodman are murdered outside the home of O J Simpson. NFL star, O J Simpson is later acquitted of the killings. In a strange turn of events O J is chased by police through Los Angeles in a televised low speed car chase.

TV stations interrupted coverage of the 1994 NBA Finals to broadcast live coverage of the pursuit, which was watched by an estimated 95 million people.

- **Gay Games opened and closed.**

The games were created as an alternative to the Olympic Games and as a way to celebrate the contributions of homosexuals to sports.

EVENTS THAT TOOK PLACE IN
JULY

Top Songs across the UK and USA charts this month:

United States: "I Swear" by All-4-One
United Kingdom: "Love Is All Around" by Wet Wet Wet

BORN IN 1994

Events that took place in the UK

- The Queen opens the SIS Building - the new MI6 headquarters, located on the River Thames.

- Tony Blair beats John Prescott and Margaret Beckett to become the new leader of the Labour Party.

- P J and Duncan - later known as 'Ant & Dec' release their single 'Let's Get Ready to Rumble'; reaching number nine in the official charts.

BORN IN 1994

Events that took place in the US

Amazon is founded by Jeff Bezos.

Fourteen fire-fighters are killed fighting a wildfire on Storm King Mountain in Colorado.

July 3rd 1994 was the deadliest day in Texas traffic history, according to the Texas Department of Public Safety.

Forty six people were killed in car crashes.

BORN IN 1994

"Forrest Gump", directed by Robert Zemeckis and starring Tom Hanks, Robin Wright, and Gary Sinise, is released.

In 1995 the film won Academy Awards Best Picture.

Former NFL running back, broadcaster and actor O.J. Simpson offers $500,000 reward for evidence of ex-wife's killer.

In their attempt to win the case, the attorneys also filed a motion accusing police of ignoring evidence that points to other possible suspects.

New York Yankees pitcher Phil Niekro strikes out Larry Parish (Texas Rangers) and becomes the ninth player to achieve 3000 MLB strikeouts.

EVENTS THAT TOOK PLACE IN

AUGUST

Top Songs across the UK and USA charts this month:

United States: "I Swear" by All-4-One
United Kingdom: "Love Is All Around" by Wet Wet Wet

BORN IN 1994

Events that took place in the UK

The new 'Sunday Trading Act 1994' allows retailers and other businesses to open on Sundays.

Although controversial at the time, this changes shopping habits over the long term.

- A new MORI poll gives Labour and its new leader, Tony Blair a massive lead over the Conservatives.

- Fire destroys Norwich Central Library destroying most of its historical records.

BORN IN 1994

- Last British troops leave Hong Kong (having been there since Sept 1841).

- British band Oasis release their debut album "Definitely Maybe", becoming the fastest-selling album ever in UK.

- Huddersfield Town move into their new all-seater Alfred McAlpine Stadium, which has an initial capacity of 16,000 and will rise to 20,000 later this year on the completion of a third stand.

  A fourth stand is also planned and would take the capacity to around 25,000.

- The Provisional Irish Republican Army declares a ceasefire.

42

BORN IN 1994

Events that took place in the US

● **The Woodstock 1994 Festival took place.**

Woodstock '94 was an American music festival celebrating the 25th anniversary of the original Woodstock festival in 1969.

○ **The 1994 – 1995 Major League Baseball strike starts – it lasts a total of 232 days.**

● **Eugene Bullard is posthumously commissioned as a Second Lieutenant in the US Air Force – 33 years after his death and 77 years after he was rejected for US Military Service in 1917.**

43

EVENTS THAT TOOK PLACE IN
SEPTEMBER

Top Songs across the UK and USA charts this month:

United States: "I'll Make Love To You" by Boyz II Men
United Kingdom: "Love Is All Around" by Wet Wet Wet

BORN IN 1994

Events that took place in the UK

- A new German discount high street supermarket, Lidl opens its doors to shoppers in the UK for the first time.

- Beloved television celebrity, Roy Castle dies at the age of 62 from lung cancer. He was best known to British viewers as the long-running presenter of the BBC children's series Record Breakers.

- On the underground, train stations Aldwych, North Weald and Ongar railway stations close permanently.

45

BORN IN 1994

Events that took place in the US

"The Shawshank Redemption", directed by Frank Darabont and starring Tim Robbins and Morgan Freeman is released.

President Bill Clinton signs the 'Violence Against Women Act 1994' and the 'Federal Assault Weapons Ban' in landmark legislation.

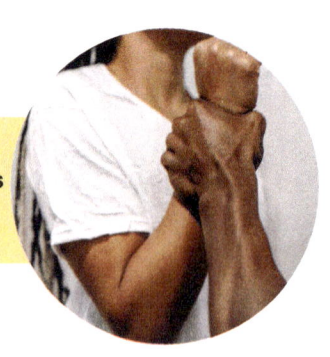

The World Series is cancelled due to a player's strike.

46

BORN IN 1994

The first episode of Friends débuts on NBC.
"Friends" TV sitcom created by David Crane and Marta Kauffman débuts on NBC, starring Jennifer Aniston, Courteney Cox, Lisa Kudrow, Matt LeBlanc, Matthew Perry and David Schwimmer.

47

BORN IN 1994

Iraq begins to move troops towards the Kuwait border resulting in America also moving troops into the area.

American troops peacefully invade Haiti to restore the legitimate elected leader to power.

11th MTV Video Music Awards: Aerosmith wins with newly-weds Michael Jackson & Lisa Marie Presley opening the show.

EVENTS THAT TOOK PLACE IN

OCTOBER

Top Songs across the UK and USA charts this month:

United States: "I'll Make Love To You" by Boyz II Men
United Kingdom: "Saturday Night" by Whigfield

BORN IN 1994

Events that took place in the UK

Unemployment continues to fall giving hope to the Conservative Party that they might be able to win next years election. Labour continues to progress.

The Rover Motor Group launched the popular Rover 100 in the UK.

In what was later known as 'The Cash for Questions Affair', Conservative Ministers Neil Hamilton and Tim Smith took cash bribes from Harrods chief Mohamed Al-Fayed to ask questions in the House of Commons.

BORN IN 1994

Korean car maker Daewoo announces that it will start selling cars directly to customers in the UK.

Pink Floyd finishes their final concert tour with a show at Earls Court in London, England.

The Division Bell Tour marked the last series of their live performances. This tour was organized to promote their album The Division Bell, which debuted just two days prior to the tour's commencement.

To celebrate this tour, the band brought out the live album Pulse in 1995. Shortly after this, the band quietly separated.

BORN IN 1994

Events that took place in the US

Steven Spielberg, Jeffrey Katzenberg and David Geffen found DreamWorks Animation.

NASA loses contact with the Magellan spacecraft. It is presumed to have burned up in Venus's atmosphere.

A man fired 29 shots at the White House in a failed attempt to assassinate President Bill Clinton.

BORN IN 1994

Statue of Sam Houston unveiled in Texas.

It was built to honour and commemorate Sam Houston's significant contribution to the history and development of Texas.

He served as the first and third President of the Republic of Texas, was a U.S. Senator after Texas joined the United States, and also served as the Governor of Texas.

The statue is not just a tribute to Houston himself, but also to the broader historical narrative of Texas.

53

EVENTS THAT TOOK PLACE IN

NOVEMBER

Top Songs across the UK and USA charts this month:

United States: "I'll Make Love To You" by Boyz II Men
United Kingdom: "Baby Come Back" by Pato Banton

BORN IN 1994

Events that took place in the UK

- First public trains run through the Channel Tunnel linking England and France under the English Channel.

- In a landmark moment for British justice, 'The Criminal Justice and Public Order Act' receives Royal Assent.

    This changed the right to silence of an accused person plus gave additional 'Stop and Search' powers to police.

- BBC1 broadcasts the first episode of much loved 'The Vicar of Dibley', written by Richard Curtis and starring Dawn French.

BORN IN 1994

- The Daily Telegraph becomes the first newspaper to launch an online edition, the Electronic Telegraph. Some 600,000 people in Britain now have access to the internet at home.

- Unemployment falls to under two and a half million for the first time since the end of 1991.

- Sparking the imagination of the British public the first UK National Lottery takes place.

BORN IN 1994

Events that took place in the US

- The first conference about the commercial potential of the 'World Wide Web' was held in San Francisco. This new exciting technology was just beginning to evolve in 1994.

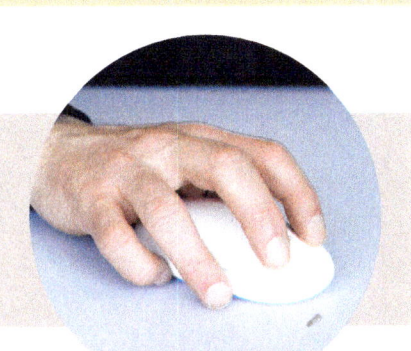

Former US President Ronald Reagan announces that he has Alzheimer.

- On November 30th, 1994, rapper Tupac Shakur was robbed and shot five times in the lobby of Quad Recording Studios in Manhattan.

BORN IN 1994

- The first internet radio broadcast was launched by a student radio station.

- The website domain name for Amazon is first registered.

- Serial killer Jeffrey Dahmer is killed in jail.

- 'The Santa Clause' movie starring Tim Allen is seen in movie theatres.

BORN IN 1994

Nirvana's live album "MTV Unplugged in New York" is released.

The album captured a moment in 90's music history, representing the peak and impending end of the grunge movement.

The album was released posthumously following Cobain's death in April 1994, adding a layer of poignancy to the recording.

EVENTS THAT TOOK PLACE IN

DECEMBER

Top Songs across the UK and USA charts this month:

United States: "I'll Make Love To You" by Boyz II Men
United Kingdom: "Let Me Be Your Fantasy" by Baby D.

BORN IN 1994

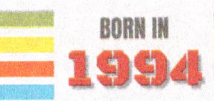

Events that took place in the UK

- In a landmark meeting, the British Government opened talks with Irish political group, Sinn Fein - the first meeting in more than 70 years.

- The Rover Motor Group ends production of the once popular Maestro and Montego ranges.

- Labour leader, Tony Blair's popularity continues to grow with latest opinion polls showing that Labour have a 39 point lead over the Conservatives.

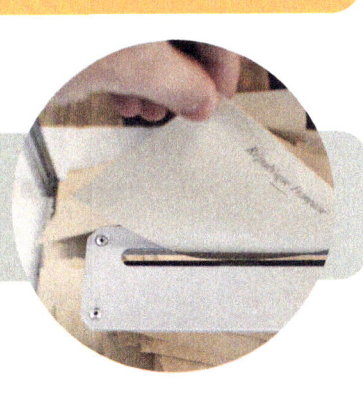

- Moors murderer, Myra Hindley who has been in prison for nearly thirty years is told that she will never be released from prison.

BORN IN 1994

Events that took place in the US

The unemployment rate drops to 5.50% - the lowest for some years.

An investigation into 'The Whitewater Scandal' begins in Washington involving property dealings by President Bill Clinton and his wife, Hillary Clinton.

5th Billboard Music Awards: Ace of Base & Mariah Carey win

Home & Garden Television débuts.

Mexico suffers a currency meltdown resulting in the Clinton Administration providing a massive financial bailout.

BORN IN 1994

The first PlayStation is released.

The PlayStation originated from a failed collaboration between Sony and Nintendo to create a CD-ROM for the Super Nintendo. After the partnership fell through, Sony decided to use its technology to create its own gaming console.

The PlayStation was one of the first video game consoles to extensively use CD-ROMs for storage, which was a significant shift from the cartridge-based systems prevalent at the time.

THE BEST AND THE WORST
1994 HAD TO OFFER

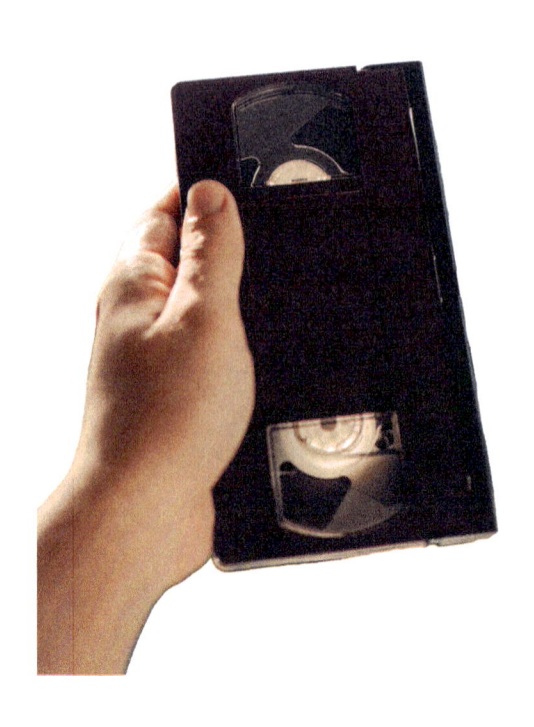

BORN IN 1994

Worlds First Satellite Digital Television Service Launched.

Netscape Navigator released quickly becoming market leader for browsing the web.

Java programming language first released from Sun Microsystems.

Scientists in Southern England estimate the oldest Europeans at 500,000 years old.

The Channel Tunnel, which took 15,000 workers over seven years to complete, and is 31 miles long opens.

Kurt Cobain commits suicide.

Lisa Marie Presley marries Michael Jackson.

The European Fighter Aircraft "Eurofighter" makes its inaugural test flight after 10 years in development.

Pink Floyd have their last performance.

Playstation is first launched.

65

TOP MUSIC ALBUMS IN THE US

1. Cracked Rear View by Hootie & The Blowfish
2. Dookie by Green Day
3. Cross Road by Bon Jovi
4. Merry Christmas by Mariah Carey
5. CrazySexyCool by TLC
6. No Need To Argue by The Cranberries
7. II by Boyz II Men
8. MTV Unplugged in New York by Nirvana
9. The Division Bell by Pink Floyd
10. Smash by The Offspring

TOP MUSIC ALBUMS IN THE UK

1. Cross Road: The Best of Bon Jovi by Bon Jovi
2. Carry On up the Charts: The Best of the Beautiful South by The Beautiful South
3. Music Box by Mariah Carey
4. Always & Forever by Eternal
5. The Division Bell by Pink Floyd
6. End of Part One: Their Greatest Hits by Wet Wet Wet
7. Monster by R.E.M.
8. Parklife by Blur
9. Live at the BBC by The Beatles
10. Steam by East 17

TOP GROSSING MOVIES IN THE US

1. The Lion King
2. Forrest Gump
3. True Lies
4. The Santa Clause
5. The Flintstones
6. Clear and Present Danger
7. Speed
8. The Mask
9. Mrs Doubtfire
10. Interview with the Vampire: The Vampire Chronicles

TOP GROSSING MOVIES IN THE UK

1. Four Weddings and a Funeral
2. The Flintstones
3. Mrs Doubtfire
4. The Lion King
5. Schindlers List
6. The Mask
7. Forrest Gump
8. True Lies
9. Pulp Fiction
10. Wayne's World 2

BORN IN 1994

SPORTING HIGHLIGHTS

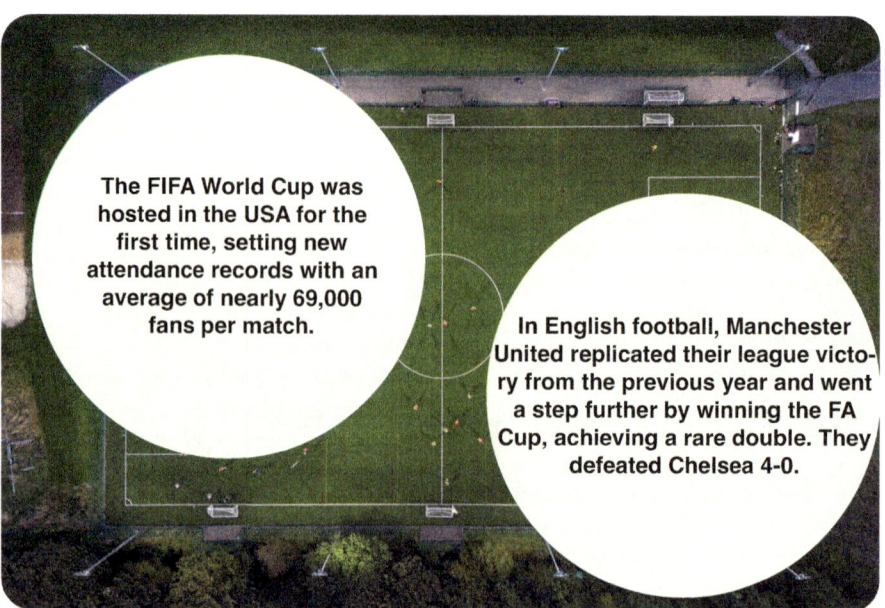

The FIFA World Cup was hosted in the USA for the first time, setting new attendance records with an average of nearly 69,000 fans per match.

In English football, Manchester United replicated their league victory from the previous year and went a step further by winning the FA Cup, achieving a rare double. They defeated Chelsea 4-0.

Major League Baseball players went on a lengthy strike that lasted from August 12 to April 2, 1995, a total of 232 days. Because of this, the Baseball World Series was cancelled that year. It was a rare occurrence that happened only once before in 1904.

It was the year of the Winter Olympics, and the drama began well before the games. Nancy Kerrigan, the then star figure skater was struck on the knee by her rival Tonya Harding's bodyguard.

BORN IN 1994

HOW MUCH DID THINGS COST IN 1994?

🇺🇸	🇬🇧
Yearly inflation rate 2.61%	Yearly inflation rate 2.55%
A gallon of gas $1.09	A gallon of petrol £0.57
Average Annual Income $37,070	Average Annual Income £20,038
Average Cost of a House $119,050	Average Cost of a House £55,925
Average Monthly Rent $375	Average Monthly Rent £230
Average Price of a New Car $12,350	Average Price of a New Car £12,207
Movie Ticket $4.08	Movie Ticket £3.25
Loaf of bread $1.59	Loaf of bread £0.54
Dozen Eggs $0.86	Dozen Eggs £0.84

BORN IN 1994

POPULAR NAMES
(IS YOURS HERE?)

Samantha   Taylor
Sarah
   Ashley
          Brittany
Amanda   Elizabeth
   Megan   Emily

Christopher   Daniel
Brandon   Matthew   Jacob
    Nicholas   Tyler
Andrew
    Joshua   Michael

BORN IN 1994

AND OF COURSE...

YOU!

HAPPY BIRTHDAY!

THANKS FOR MAKING 1994 SO SPECIAL!

THE END.

KNOW SOMEONE WHO WOULD LOVE THIS BOOK?

GET THEM A COPY!

Printed in Great Britain
by Amazon